BRITAIN IN OLD PI

POOLE

ANN NORBURY

ALAN SUTTON PUBLISHING LIMITED

Alan Sutton Publishing Limited
Phoenix Mill · Far Thrupp · Stroud
Gloucestershire · GL5 2BU

First published 1995

Copyright © Ann Norbury, 1995

Cover photographs: front, children with their
tricycle, *c.* 1890; back, a postcard from Poole,
c. 1903.

British Library Cataloguing in Publication Data.
A catalogue record for this book is available from
the British Library.

ISBN 0-7509-0933-1

Typeset in 9/10 Sabon.
Typesetting and origination by
Alan Sutton Publishing Limited.
Printed in Great Britain by
WBC Limited, Bridgend.

Contents

Egeria, *c*. 1870. This two-masted schooner with a square stern was launched on 18 May 1865 from the Hamworthy yard of Thomas Wanhill. Her gross tonnage was 74.89, beam 19.25 ft, length 98.4 ft, draught 10 ft. Owned from 1865 to 1895 by Mr John Mulholland MP (1819–95), 1st Baron Dunleath, she belonged to the Royal Yacht Squadron from 1865 to 1898, but was broken up at Gosport (Hants) on 12 August 1899. Her racing career was excellent: in her maiden race, she beat *Aline*. She twice beat *Livornia*, purpose-built for the America Cup Race, and won the Queen's Cup at Cowes five times between 1865 and 1881. An excellent heavy weather boat, she is shown here on the starboard tack, a square racing flag at her main mast head.

Introduction

By a quirk of fate, Poole is not only a port and a resort, it is also a unique historical entity, because in 1568, for the only time in her long reign, Queen Elizabeth I granted county status to a town. The County of the Town of Poole bore its title proudly until 1974, and will do so again from 1997, as the Borough and County of the Town of Poole.

Poole has double tides and two coastlines: one to the open sea and beaches of Poole Bay, the other to the large natural harbour in which the original old town lies. Its beauties are many and varied, and photographers have practised their art here since at least 1851, when 'George Marks, 37, unmarried, photographic artist' was recorded by a Census enumerator at the house of Ann Palk, in the High Street.

At that time, Poole was recovering from two or three decades of recession largely due to the loss of much of its lucrative Newfoundland trade, together with a drastic reduction in profits from smuggling because of a stronger Preventive Service, and other causes. The old town was shabby, but new businesses were growing, and people were adapting to new ways of doing things.

Those who could, moved out of the crowded old town into the more spacious new suburbs of Longfleet and Parkstone, to the east of Poole. Developers created new residential estates, which have continued to grow, where there had been only smallholdings, farms, potteries, brickworks, a mill, and a scattering of houses. This trend has continued, with large parts of the older areas also undergoing redevelopment.

From the early twentieth century, improved transport, seaside excursions, recreational boating, houseboats and beach bungalows brought new life to Poole's harbour and coastline. This was an extension in scale of what already existed, as Poole has long been a centre for many types of pleasure boating, as well as mercantile trade.

Yachts built between the 1840s and 1860s in Wanhill's yard at Hamworthy were world famous for their sailing capabilities, none more so than *Egeria*. Also, when other forms of marine work dwindled, many Poole men sailed as masters, mates or crew aboard large yachts, sometimes combining this with a traditional family fishing business. Indeed, in 1911, E. Keble Chatterton wrote that the hulls and sails of Poole fishing cutters were more akin to yachts than was usual for work boats.

Then, as now, Poole people gave their time to voluntary organizations, such as the lifeboat service, fire brigade, Scouts and Guides, churches, chapels and community groups. The many surviving photographs of the fund-raising events run by these groups, such as outings, fêtes, carnivals and sports days, testify to their popularity.

When one thinks of the long hours worked at the turn of the century – a local man campaigned for a once-a-week early closing day of 5 p.m. – and the physical labour required in domestic chores, it is amazing how much energy was put into leisure activities. It took effort and ingenuity to devise and make tableaux, floats and costumes for the various annual events, but up to 1914 there seems to have been no shortage of entrants.

After 1918, trips in paddlesteamers and charabancs became even more popular; trams, cars, lorries and buses were no longer a novelty; aeroplanes came and went, some taking aerial photographs. Radio and talking films became popular entertainment, along with the gramophone, and eventually television. Businesses grew up to service new demands, or to create them.

Often, pictures were taken only when places were changing, so there is scant record of how they had been. For instance, clay from the Poole area has been used for centuries in potteries, but there are few photographs of the old workings. Local potteries used to make thousands of drainpipes, tiles, architectural wares and domestic articles, to meet the building boom here and abroad. Poole Pottery continues, but many other firms have vanished almost without photographic trace.

Over the years, many photographs have been taken of Poole and Hamworthy Quays, and shipping in the Harbour, as they have of such landmarks as the Custom House, the Guildhall, the Town Cellars, and 'the seaside'. Harder to come by are pictures of people working, the interiors of their homes, and the residential parts of Poole. Perhaps you have some that Poole Museum could copy, and share with others, to give a clearer idea of vanished Poole?

Within the limits of what is available, I have tried to give this book the flavour of life in Poole from about the middle of the nineteenth century to the middle of this, and hope that you will enjoy browsing through it. If you are a newcomer to the area, you could use it to help you explore the beauties of Poole. If you know the area and people whose roots are here, I hope it will give you shared hours of reminiscences about 'the old days', which you can pass on to others.

Now I would like to take you on a tour of Poole over the past century or so, show you some of the places in it, introduce you to people of Poole and give you a glimpse of their lives – their work, their leisure, the events in which they were involved.

Let us start with a map of 1928 to familiarize ourselves with the area. The photographs that follow will, I hope, illustrate the changes that have taken place in Poole over the last hundred years or so. We shall end with a day at the seaside, complete with cream tea, postcards and souvenirs.

Section One

MAPS

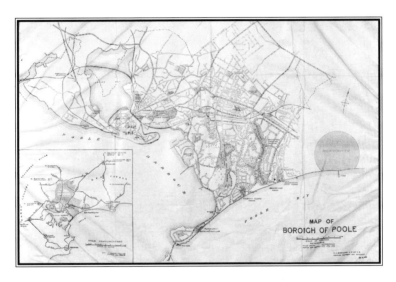

This map, drawn in 1928 by the Borough Engineer, E.J. Goodacre, shows the borough boundaries, and road and rail links, with a small scale inset map of the area around Poole. Although lacking road names, it is a useful guide to how parts of the borough relate to each other geographically and the location of now defunct rail lines shown in some of the following photographs.

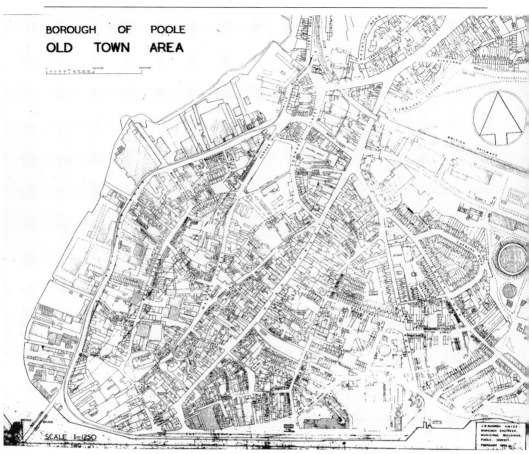

J.R. Barron, the Borough Engineer, drew up this map of the old town in 1952, in preparation for clearance and redevelopment – a new road from Hunger Hill to the Bridge is outlined. Except around Poole Pottery, there is little change from a 1902 map. The railway lines between the Quay and the station can be clearly seen, as can the two parts of the gas works.

THAMES, PARADISE AND SALISBURY STREETS

Watergate, c. 1890. Until reclamation in Tudor times, the shoreline was at the back of houses in Thames Street (then called Key or Quay Street). This gate was in a thick wall at the rear of property adjoining the Town Cellars, which have since been bisected by Thames Street. One portion of the Town Cellars is now part of a museum, while the other is part of a public house. The St Clement Inn has been demolished.

Poole Quay, *c.* 1905. The tower of St James' Church rises above buildings in Thames Street, which is flanked by the Harbour Office and the Town Cellars. A horse-drawn cab from The London Hotel (High Street) and a large car await their passengers, probably from an overdue paddle-steamer.

Harbour Office, *c.* 1900. The colonnades were added to support an extension on the first floor of the building, used as a reading room and known as the Town House, with its own entrance on the side. In the foreground are the Town Cellars, with one of several public water pumps.

Paradise Street, *c.* 1900. This is a rare view towards the High Street, with a glimpse of house fronts which were later converted to shops. Oakley's warehouse is in use, its shutters open towards the Custom House.

Maritime Museum, *c.* 1980. The Town Cellars has become a museum; behind it, the corner of Salisbury Street has been redeveloped. In Paradise Street, Oakley's warehouse is closed.

Town Cellars, *c.* 1970. The old Wool House or King's Hall, which had been a sort of bonded warehouse for goods of the Staple, later became known as the Town Cellars. In 1910 it was bought by Oakley Brothers for general storage and given by them to Poole Corporation in 1929.

Town Cellars, *c.* 1975. When the Council decided to transform the old Town Cellars into a museum, archaeological examination revealed that the main walls of the building date from about 1300; it was altered and reroofed about a century later, and altered again when cut through by Thames Street in about 1786.

Maritime Museum interior, 1976. The Town Cellars became a focal point for the maritime history of Poole, depicting its flora and fauna, and the people and craft that used it.

The junction of High Street and Salisbury Street, 1923. Behind the Town Cellars and Oakley's warehouse, Scaplen's Court presents a rather dilapidated Georgian frontage to the High Street.

Scaplen's Court after storm damage, 1924. Note the bricks stacked in front, after demolition was started to provide lorry parking. Many bricks and roof tiles were sold to a Sussex firm before the building was preserved for the town.

Doorway to 'best parlour', 1924. The room's cornice and wainscotting bore fine quality carving in similar style. Its tenant, Mrs Adey, was eighty years old, and could remember alterations which had been made since she was born here.

West end of Upper Hall, 1924. An ancient panelled partition in chestnut extended from the left towards the worked stone doorway of the solar. The arched wooden door frame in it predated the steep stairs leading to the attics, which were made in the eighteenth century.

Lower Hall, Scaplen's Court, 1924. On the left can be seen a bricked-up doorway to the west wing, and partial demolition has revealed a huge early fireplace behind a Victorian range.

Solar roof, 1924. This woodwork was made to be seen from the rooms below. Chamfered braces form continuous arches. Each roof slope has four purlins, with two pairs of curved and chamfered wind braces to each bay between them, laid in an alternating pattern. Little attic bedrooms can be glimpsed through the doorway in the photograph above.

Scaplen's Court, 1950s. After the war, Scaplen's Court needed to be refurbished. When money and materials were available, it was closed to the public, and reopened again as a museum in 1959.

Scaplen's Court courtyard. Damaged portions of the fabric were stabilized, but not repaired. Changes in use over time are clearly shown in these walls.

Scaplen's Court reconstructed, 1987. The old building was re-roofed, gaps in the walls were filled, and the front bay rebuilt on its foundations. Where necessary, new floors were laid, and a wider staircase was installed in the courtyard. A specially commissioned stained-glass window was put in the first floor bay, with colourful symbols associated with Poole's history, such as fish, boats, nets and a dolphin.

HIGH STREET AND MOUNT STREET

*Norton Building, c. 1900. A few years earlier, John
Norton gave the town this building in Mount Street
(now Lagaland Street) to house a public library,
museum, gymnasium and art school. Its central
location was enhanced when first the tram terminus
and then the bus station were sited nearby.*

Heraldry display, *c.* 1950. This exhibition at the old museum was probably staged when Henry Harbin School published its book, *Poole Heraldry*.

Old Museum, *c.* 1950. This general view of the museum exhibition also shows the windows and pillars in the Norton Building.

Mount Street Hall, *c*. 1891. Near the Norton Building, this hall was built for the Plymouth Brethren at a cost of £800, and opened on 11 February 1891; George Hawes snr and Charles Ashton were founders. The first wedding at the Hall was of George Joseph Hawes and Jane Ann Davis, on 28 September 1892.

Plymouth Brethren, *c*. 1890. Before the Mount Street Hall was built, local Brethren used to meet in a large outbuilding in this garden, behind George Hawes' High Street shop. Jesse Carter (founder of Poole Pottery) belonged to this sect.

High Street, 1901. Hawes & Hawes moved to Poole in 1882. Here, they have expanded from 101 and 103 (formerly 75 and 77) to include 105 and 107. It is easy to see that these buildings were originally houses, refronted at ground floor level.

High Street, c. 1903. Mr Hawes has unified his shop front, making it into a replica of his previous shop in Fulham. About a dozen of the shop assistants lived in 101–3, the Hawes family lived in 105, and 107 was let. One of the town's old mulberry trees is in the garden.

High Street, 1960s. Before moving to the shopping centre, chain stores as well as local shops were in the High Street. Marks & Spencer occupied 105–7, and Tesco 101–3, all of which had been Hawes & Hawes. Hawkes shoe shop remains at no. 99.

High Street, October 1938. 'Mrs Eti Long of Chapel Lane, snapped near St Paul's Church. 3 for 1s.' This street photographer was stationed near the churchyard railings, looking towards the post office and Mount Street.

No. 46 High Street, *c.* 1905. This house was built partly in the sixteenth century, extended and divided in the eighteenth century, and modified in about 1840. The upstairs sitting room has a curved ceiling, because of the truss roof, similar to houses in Castle Street and to Scaplen's Court. Note the elegant gas light over the table, and the reflections in the mirror, including a person – shadowy because he moved.

Section Four

CASTLE STREET, QUAYS AND BRIDGE

Poole, c. 1585. This is an artist's impression of the area around Fish Street (now Castle Street), with a small part of the High Street in the foreground, showing houses similar to those found behind later façades when the area was redeveloped in the 1960s, and also 'garden grounds', which are frequently referred to in old Poole deeds.

Castle Street, 1960s. The rear of nos 12–26 is seen here in winter from the corner of Caroline Row and Strand Street, with the railings of Strand Street Mission in the foreground.

Castle Street, 1960s. The rear of nos 16–26, showing the mulberry trees in leaf behind the stone cottages and outbuildings. These trees were planted for silk production.

No. 20 Castle Street, interior, 1960s. While the buildings were being stripped, these fine doorways, vast fireplace and the altered floor level were revealed.

No. 19 Castle Street, 1960s. The last remaining wall of the house clearly shows its tie and spur beams, and wattle and daub construction, as well as a blocked sixteenth-century doorway.

Poole Quay, looking from the Jolly Sailor public house towards the old Custom House, 1874. On the right is the junction with Fish Street (Castle Street), where the Mission to Seamen was opened in 1860.

Poole Quay, c. 1910. Craft are drying their sails near John Carter's warehouse, which used to be the Britannia Inn, between the Poole Arms and the Portsmouth Hoy. Poole Pottery's kilns are on the right.

Cargo, 1940s. A fleet of lorries and a line of empty rail trucks foretell a busy morning ahead on Poole Quay, near Poole Pottery.

'Le Havre'. A line was laid from the station goods yard to Poole Quay in the 1870s. This was one of the engines used on that route until 1962, when the lines were removed.

The Custom House, July 1937. This is the view from the Harbour Office eastwards. A Custom House stood on this site for centuries, with the King's Beam outside to weigh imported or exported goods for taxation. There is now a new office in Hamworthy.

Family drive, *c.* 1910. 'Mrs Preston going for her afternoon drive, with baby Doris, and Lily.' The Preston family came from Brockenhurst to run the Shipwright Arms, where this was taken. Opposite are the Harbour Office and Custom House on Poole Quay.

Between the Quays, *c.* 1920. The PS *Wareham Queen* is alongside Hamworthy Quay, close to the ferry steps and waiting room. Opposite is Poole Quay, at its junction with the High Street.

Hamworthy Quay, *c.* 1925. A Scandinavian timber ship is about to unload, as the first horse-drawn cart arrives. There have been changes in the yard since we saw the *Wareham Queen* moored in the same position.

Poole Harbour, *c.* 1905. This view between *Gannet* and the paddle-steamer *Telegraph* was taken from Hamworthy Quay, and shows Poole Quay from the Harbour Office along to the bend near the Victoria Steam Mill, and on towards the bridge.

Between the Quays, *c.* 1900. Looking across towards Hamworthy from the bend on Poole Quay near the Victoria Steam Mill, an evening calm has replaced the bustle of loading and unloading. There is still only a single track along Poole Quay for the railway.

Small boats at Ham Quay, *c*. 1900. Yachts and tenders lie close to Hamworthy Quay, east of the Shipwright Arms. On the right, larger vessels are alongside Poole Quay, near the Victoria Steam Mill.

Poole Quay, *c*. 1914. From near the Shipwright Arms, we can see beyond the second bridge into Holes Bay, and also a variety of craft alongside Poole Quay.

The Quay, 1951. The crisp winter morning gives an excellent view across to Poole Bridge and to Hamworthy, showing everything blanketed in snow.

Timber yard, *c*. 1890. Logs are stacked in Sydenham's yard, near the bridge at Hamworthy, and Poole Quay bristles with masts and spars, with the long stack of a steam tug raised among them.

The second Poole Bridge, *c.* 1914. This winter view shows the old Toll Collector's house on the left, at the Poole bridgehead, close to Sydenham's timber yard. The second bridge was a swing bridge, opened in 1885 and replaced in 1927.

Mayor Herbert Carter is shown cutting the ribbon to symbolically open Poole's third bridge, 9 March 1927.

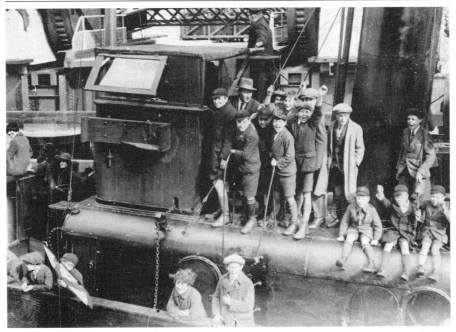

First traffic through the new bridge, 1927. The tug *Talbot* was one of many craft that chugged through the new bridge at its first opening, with flags flying and whistles and hooters blowing, to the cheers and waves of people aboard and ashore.

Crowds at the bridge opening, 1927. This is a small part of the crowd which came to see the first traffic through Poole's new lifting bridge.

FAMILY AND FRIENDS

Adelaide Adey, c. 1855. On 29 November 1855
Adelaide married John Guy at St Peter's Church,
Parkstone. She was born on 17 March 1832, daughter of
Hannah and William Adey of Poole.

Sion William Wilkins, 1883. Sion Wilkins was a Poole master mariner, mostly engaged in the Newfoundland trade. This was a hard life by his time, as competition was intense and the rewards uncertain.

Edward Wanhill, c. 1880. Descendants of the Wanhill shipbuilding firm remained in this area until the 1960s. The early deaths of Thomas Wanhill and his brother James Manlaws Wanhill, and some financial problems, meant that the family was no longer involved with building yachts or other craft.

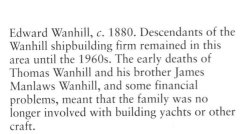

Alice Mary Wetton, *c.* 1890. This *carte de visite* was made at about the time of her marriage to William Kelley of Clapper Farm.

William Frederick Kelley, *c.* 1890. This picture was taken at about the time of his marriage to Alice Wetton. William took over the family farm at Longfleet when his father could no longer run it. They moved to 12 Wimborne Road in the 1920s, after the farm was sold.

Elias Harris (1822–93). The son of William and Charlotte (née Budd), he married Frances Maria Budden. Their daughter, Annie Sophie, married Frank Spinney of Poole, and raised a large family.

Teachers, 1893. These ladies all taught at the British School, Skinner Street. Seated on the left is Isobel Poole (1871–1955), who married her cousin Isaiah John Poole (1859–1917) in August 1893. Her sister May (1878–1961) is in front.

Poole Working Men's Social Club, *c.* 1902. Fred Chisman, on the right of the front row, played football for Bournemouth Gas & Water Company, and the Dorset County Team. T. and M. Cartridge and Bill Chisman are behind him.

Mother and baby, 1901. Daisy Sybil Victoria Beament, born 1901, is on her mother's lap, wearing the christening robe that served several generations; it is now in the Museum Collection.

The Allen family, *c.* 1902. William Allen (1857–1940) ran one of the Hamworthy boatyards opposite Poole Quay, after he and two of his brothers served their apprenticeships at Meadus' yard. Back row, left to right: Gertrude (b. 1890, m. Mills, then Moses), Sarah (1887–1905), Mabel (b. 1885, m. Barnes). Centre row: Elsie (b. 1892, m. Brixey), William, Bessie (b. 1889, m. Tilsed, then MacIntosh), Ellen (née Smith, b. 1860), Hilda (b. 1894, m. Goff). Front row: Dorothy ('Dulcie', b. 1897, m. Tiley), Ivy (b. 1899, m. Kendall).

The Bishop family, 1870s. The lady on the left, with the teacup, is Mrs Benjamin Bishop, wife of the photographer; ranged at the back are four of their children. The lady on the right is a member of the Sydenham family of Poole and Bournemouth.

Invitation, 1903. George and Sarah Curtis married on 3 August 1843. By 1851 they had a son and three daughters; a second son was born in December 1852, but lived for only fifteen weeks.

Longfleet Infants' School, *c*. 1900. Class 2 are obviously wearing their Sunday best for the photographer.

Longfleet Girls' School, c. 1913. Standards V, VI and VII were combined for this picture. Louisa Kelley is third from the left in the second row from the back.

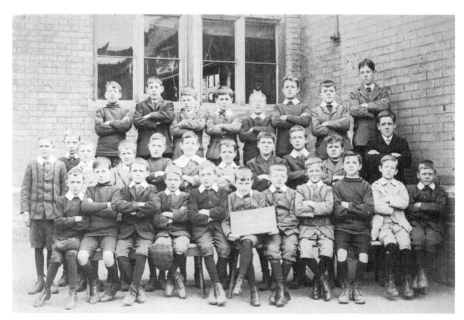

Longfleet Boys' School, 1912. Reginald George White was a pupil in Group 2a at this time. He married Louisa Kelley, who attended the girls' part of the school.

Minister and deacons, 1904. Skinner Street Independent Chapel was deeply involved with the lives of many Poole families. Back row, left to right: Mr J. Alfred Hawkes, Mr J. Reynish, Mr Lisby, Mr Green. Front row: Mr George ?, Mr Mate, Rev. Frederick Hirst, Mr Buckley, Rev. Mr White.

DEACONS, March, 1949.
H. C. Christopher, H. C. Cutler, B. A. Dacombe, A. E. Brown.

Skinner Street Independent Chapel, 1949. Many of these deacons, and their minister, were involved with providing help and comforts for servicemen and evacuees during the war. Back row, left to right: H.C. Christopher, H.C. Cutler, B.A. Dacombe, A.E. Brown. Front row: Miss J. Goodfellow, Mrs W.G. Curran, H.E. Best, Rev. F.O. Brown MA, W. Knight, Miss B. Freeborn.

Poole Grammar School, 1937. This picture of Form IIIC was taken in May, the final term in which the school was mixed. Back row, left to right: Niada Francis, Norman Pipler, Beryl Hitching, -?-, Phyllis ?, John Gale, -?-, Ian Hall, Joan Ballam, Rita Goree ('London Hotel'). Third row: Kathleen Prior, ? Barfoot, Pamela Dumper (Upton), -?-, Doreen ?, -?-, Hetty Porter, Robert Mitchell, Margaret Honeybun, Christine Carter. Second row: ? Herridge, Margery Dean (hairdressers, Towngate Street), Mr Froud, Mr Greenfield (headmaster), Jean Bell, Raymond Welsh, Joan Day, Olive Lacy. Front row: ? Ayles/Isles, -?-, Peter ?.

David Lord RNR, DCM, 1916. David Henry Lord, born on 18 May 1899, became a naval Boy Signaller in May 1915. In July 1916 the drifter in which he served was attacked and sunk; the survivors were in the water for eight hours before being rescued, after two of them swam nearly 2 miles for help. After convalescing from his ordeal in hospital, Lord was invalided out of the RNR in October 1916. He died in 1957 aged 58.

Poole Soldiers Home Committee, c. 1918. On the right of the second row, behind the kneeling soldiers, is Alice Kelley (née Wetton) of Clapper Farm, Longfleet.

New war memorial, Poole Park, November 1927. Miss Margaret Llewellin, who had recently been appointed Girl Guide Commissioner for Poole, is handing a poppy wreath to HRH Edward, Prince of Wales (later King Edward VIII).

Workers' playtime, 1945. These four girls had something to smile about: the war was over.

Lt.-Gen. Sir R.S.S. Baden-Powell, Bart, GCVO, GCMG, KCB, FRGS (1857–1941), 21 May 1929. This picture was taken in the High Street just after he had received the Freedom of Poole, as is shown by the Freedom casket carried behind him. Robert Baden-Powell had strong links with Poole. In 1907 his first experimental Scout camp was held on Brownsea Island; he married Olave Soames at Parkstone in 1912, and their son was christened there in 1914. The Freedom of Poole was conferred on Lady Baden-Powell on 20 May 1950, the first instance of both husband and wife receiving the honour.

Section Six

EVENTS, SPORTS AND HOBBIES

*1st Poole Boy Scouts, c. 1908. Among those practising ambulance drill is Bill Eason, a
keen sportsman and athlete, who joined Poole Pottery's faience department drawing office in
1909. The Scout movement started with a camp on Brownsea Island, organized by Baden-
Powell, which comprised a mix of boys from public schools and local council schools. The
lives of many people must have been saved during the First World War through the
knowledge and skills gained in the Scouts and Guides.*

Scout kitchen, *c.* 1912. Reginald White is among those making sandwiches in this example of team work.

Temperance Fête, June 1906. These children are posed in Poole Park, with their coloured ribbons twined around the maypole.

Horse parade, 1903. Poole Park seems to have turned into the Wild West for this stereoscopic picture. A companion view of cowboys needs conservation.

Sports Day, 10 June 1908. There is not much evidence of 'ladies in front' in this picture. The large number of boys and youths in front suggests that a local hero was being challenged.

Poole Volunteers Band, *c*. 1895. Live music was an important part of events, and bands were much in demand on high days and holidays, as well as for Sunday concerts in the Park.

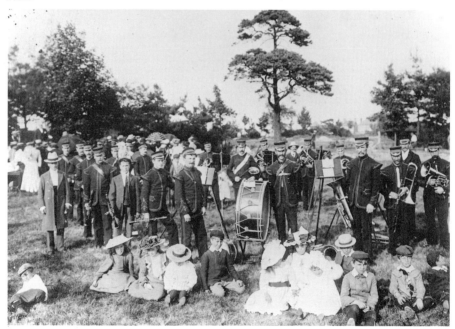

Poole Band, *c*. 1900. There is a large crowd at Whitecliff listening to the band. Note the older style of uniforms.

Poole Town Band, 1911. In 1938 the Council officially thanked Mr Richardson for playing in the band for the past fifty years on Mayor's Sunday and other occasions.

Hospital Sunday, *c.* 1905. Poole Town Band is shown leading the procession along Ashley Road, Parkstone, near the junction with Edward Road.

Fishermen's Regatta, *c.* 1910. People thronged the quayside near Poole Pottery, while others tried for a ringside seat in small boats, but the man standing on the deck of a moored boat probably had the best view of the fun.

Poole Carnival Queen, 17 June 1914. People worked hard to enjoy themselves, as shown by this elaborate tableau. Only weeks later, the First World War broke out.

Poole Carnival Queen, 1930s. Young Zena Davis and her attendants are shown in all their finery. Zena, a member of a long-established Poole seafaring family, was Queen again a few years later.

The Mayor going to Poole Carnival, c. 1933. Mr Field drove the mayoral car in many processions, with the mace bearer standing beside him.

Mayoral Carnival float, 14 July. Here, the Mayor and Admiral of the Port is in the good ship *Poole*, with Mr Field at the wheel. Note the model boats on the windscreen. There are also model vehicles on the bonnet, in what appears to be a potential traffic jam with a coal train.

Poole Carnival, *c.* 1912. Herbert Saunders was Sheriff in 1907, and ran a grocery shop at 20 High Street. Here, his son Herbert Charles is dressed as a blackamoor, riding the delivery horse, Blackie.

Poole Carnival, *c.* 1913. Poole Rowing Club have borrowed fire crew uniforms and an engine for their tableau.

Poole Carnival stand, *c.* 1925. Radio was a novelty; the BBC had started in 1922 on 2LO, and in 1923 Bournemouth radio station broadcast on 6BM, all of which was excellent for C.H. Gould's new radio business in Towngate Street.

Towngate Street, 1920s. William Gould enjoyed window dressing, as shown by this lavish display for Poole Carnival, which, by the number above the spotlight, seems to be part of a competition.

Peace celebrations, 19 July 1919. This date was designated as a national day of celebration. Here, parties of children are walking along Kingland Road and into Poole Park.

Poole Model Yacht Club float, 1902. These fine models must have taken many hours to build, and would have been the envy of most of the small boys who saw them.

Coronation tableau 'The Bakers', 1902. Henry Burden & Sons had a bakery at 203 High Street, Longfleet.

Beating the Bounds, 1920s. As Admiral of the Port, the Mayor periodically goes in ceremonial style to set places to read Poole's ancient charters and claim jurisdiction. The party here has stopped for tea at Harvey's, Sandbanks.

Beating the Bounds, 1930s. Poole Band are on duty again for this event, which had been revived in 1921 after a lapse during Victorian times.

Cycle race in Poole Park, *c.* 1918. The Council had laid out a special track for cycle races, which was regularly used by Poole Wheelers.

Tug-o'-war, *c.* 1900. These houses had a grandstand view of the tussle, but some youngsters have scrambled up to sit on the high wall.

Punt fishing, *c.* 1920. For hundreds of years, shallow craft like this were much used in the harbour for fishing, eeling and wildfowling.

Tennis in Poole Park. Friends of the Kelley and White families watch mixed doubles playing.

Bournemouth Gas & Water Co. FC, 1913–14. The club were winners outright this season. Bert Read, who was awarded a Military Medal in 1917, played for them and for Longfleet St Mary.

Hamworthy Engineering Apprentices Team, 1917–18. Back row, left to right: Hawkins, Jacobs, Compton, Hunt, Tucker. Centre row: Maxted, Tucker, Bridle. Front row: Hawkins, Goater, -?- (Belgian), Hawkyard, Smith.

Poole Ladies' Football Team, 1921. Posed in front of the changing rooms are, back row, left to right: P. Master (trainer), Daisy Edwards, -?-, -?-, Percy Ford or Bob Cobb. Centre row: Mr Cobb, Lily Cruise, Bessie Hunt, Lil Brown, -?-, -?-, -?-. Front row: Elsie Hookway, -?-, -?-.

Poole Football Club, 1925–6. This was obviously a winning season, as shown by the Bankes Charity Cup, the Dorset Senior Cup (Western League Division 2), and the Dorset League Cup. The club held their annual dance on 3 March 1926, and had plenty to celebrate.

Cricket in Poole Park. In 1902 Poole Council agreed with Mr Manfield, Secretary of Dorset County Cricket Club, to spend up to £300 on alterations to the ground, so that County matches could be played there.

Henry Harbin School team, 1958–9. The jubilation of this young team was ably caught by D.R. Davis of Hamworthy. [Published with his kind permission.]

'The den', *c.* 1920. 'My studio and Jimmy May, with *Winifred*'s new topsail in the foreground.'

'The den', *c.* 1925. His love of the sea is obvious, but this man was also a keen amateur photographer, and took several of the photos in this book.

WORK

Richard Hayes, 1950. Seen here mending his nets, holding the shuttle in his mouth while both hands were full, this local fisherman served on the lifeboat for forty years, mostly as coxswain, maintaining a strong family tradition of such service.

PS *Wareham Queen*. An unusual view across a workshop roof shows this paddle-steamer on the Patent Slipway at Hamworthy. Her owner and captain was Charles Steele.

The launch of *Asterope*. This vessel has just come off the slipway of a Hamworthy yard and is manoeuvring in a confined space. Note the spars used as 'legs'.

Poole Quay, 1950s. Messrs James and Hitchcock, two of the pilots who guided vessels through the harbour, are pictured near the ferry steps.

Wappy, 1950s. This two-masted ex-Baltic trader was the home of chief harbour pilot Mr James and his family, until they sold her and moved to Fernside Road. In 1982 *Wappy* was in Oakland, near San Francisco, USA.

PS *Monarch*, *c.* 1930. She was a familiar sight on the route to Weymouth, and in mid-season would be gently set on the sands there, so that weed could be scrubbed from her bottom, as shown here.

West Quay, *c.* 1890. This freighter has come through the old swing bridge to unload its cargo of barrels at the South Coast Shipping Company's wharf.

The barkyard, *c.* 1895. This yard was part of a Hamworthy tannery: bark was stripped from timber offcuts and stacked ready for use in tanning leather.

Gas Works, *c.* 1950. This view clearly shows the transporter which carried coal and coke from the harbourside into the Works. The Quay Hotel is now on this site.

The Quay, *c.* 1890. Horse-drawn carts queue outside Belben's Flour Mill, near Castle Street, waiting to load their sacks.

Belben's Flour Mill, 1900. The entire workforce seems to have been mustered for the photographer.

Mill wheel, Witchampton. This massive wheel was made at the Poole Foundry, Thames Street, as shown by its makers' plate.

'Western Pride', 1963. This steam engine, made by Robert Stephenson & Hawthorne Ltd, was in regular use at Hamworthy coal depot.

Branksea Pottery, *c.* 1860. The Branksea Clay & Pottery Company was founded by Col. Waugh in the 1850s, on the most up-to-date lines. After his bankruptcy, it was run by trustees, then a new owner, but closed in 1887.

Alder Hills, *c.* 1925. The Sharp Jones Bourne Valley Pottery used this engine to bring clay from its pits to the Branksome works. Here, 'Mars' is about to cross Alder Road from the west, with the driver 'Speck' at the engine doorway.

Hamworthy, *c.* 1890. This was the Patent Architectural Pottery in Blandford Road, whose chimney dominated the skyline for years. It was established in 1855 and bought by Carter & Co. (Poole Pottery), in 1895.

North Street, September 1928. Butler & Sons are extending their shop front along the side. In the background is Towngate Street, now part of Hunger Hill Roundabout.

GEORGE JENNINGS

RESPECTFULLY INVITES THE ATTENTION OF ARCHITECTS AND SURVEYORS TO HIS

SANITARY AND BUILDING APPLIANCES.

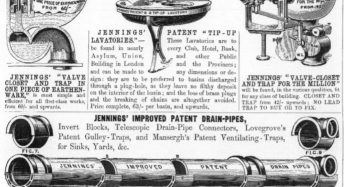

JENNINGS' "VALVE CLOSET AND TRAP IN ONE PIECE OF EARTHEN-WARE," is most simple and efficient for all first-class works, from 60/- and upwards.

JENNINGS' "TIP-UP LAVATORIES."— These Lavatories are to be found in nearly every Club, Hotel, Bank, Asylum, Union, and other Public Building in London and the Provinces; and can be made to any dimensions or design: they are to be preferred to basins discharged through a plug-hole, as they leave no filthy deposit on the interior of the basin; and the loss of brass plugs and the breaking of chains are altogether avoided. Price complete, 63/- per basin, and upwards.

JENNINGS' "VALVE-CLOSET AND TRAP FOR THE MILLION" will be found, in the various qualities, fit for any class of building. CLOSET AND TRAP from 42/- upwards; NO LEAD TRAP TO BUY OR TO FIX.

JENNINGS' IMPROVED PATENT DRAIN-PIPES, Invert Blocks, Telescopic Drain-Pipe Connectors, Lovegrove's Patent Gulley-Traps, and Mansergh's Patent Ventilating-Traps, for Sinks, Yards, &c.

JENNINGS' PATENT LIPPED URINALS, for Works of every Class. As these are generally known and appreciated, it is only necessary to remind Architects when drawing their Specifications, to state "Jennings' Patent Flat Back" or "Angular Lipped Urinals."

JENNINGS' PATENT AIR-CHAMBER SMOKE-FLUES.—By the use of these Flues, the Warming and Ventilation of Buildings is ensured with economy of fuel, as no heat can pass up the Chimney wastefully without raising the Temperature of the Air-supply of the rooms in which they are employed.

JENNINGS' IMPROVED PATENT BONDING-BRICK FOR THE CONSTRUCTION OF HOLLOW WALLS.—Walls so constructed, render Houses Warm in Winter, Cool in Summer, and Dry at all times. These improved Patent Bond-Bricks are well worthy the attention of Architects, as by their use, underground Works are strengthened and rendered perfectly dry; they also keep the faces of Area and other retaining Walls free from the influence of the moist ground abutting upon them.

JENNINGS' PATENT AIR-BRICKS can be had of any Size, from 9in. x 3in., up to 18in. x 18in., and of any Shade of Colour, from light Cream up to a dark Brown, Glazed or Unglazed. These Bricks are not only cheaper than Iron, but they are stronger and require no painting.

JENNINGS' PATENT SHOP SHUTTER-SHOE & FASTENER shoe and secure Shutters without a Bar. Reference to Eight Thousand Shop Fronts.

JENNINGS' PATENT PUMPS, Sluice-Valves, Fire and other Cocks, Improved Gas and Water-Pipes, by the use of which a length of Gas or Water-Pipe can be removed from any Fittings without trouble. These and many other things can be seen at the Works.

These Patent Pipes are sold at the same price as the Common Socket Pipes.

PALACE WHARF, STANGATE, LONDON, S.E.;

DRAIN-PIPE, BRICK AND TERRA-COTTA WORKS, SOUTH WESTERN POTTERY, PARKSTONE, POOLE, DORSET.

Advertisement, *c.* 1900. George Jennings' South Western Pottery advertised extensively and traded successfully for many years. In the 1960s it was demolished for housing, its site recalled by road names such as Potters Way, Pottery Road, Jennings Road, and South Western Crescent.

Pottery yard, *c.* 1900. Finished goods were stored here, ready to meet orders. Examples of mouldings, finials, chimney pots and drainage pipes can be seen.

Clay pit, *c.* 1900. This pit was worked for South Western Pottery, and shows tramlines and trucks used to take the clay to their works. Note the makeshift buffer in the foreground, left, where there is a steep drop.

South Western Pottery, 1960s. This picture of the interior was taken before demolition; this is probably a store loft. Moulds and the paraphernalia for filling and moving them are scattered about.

Ice cream seller, 1950. Luigi Zollo was much loved by schoolchildren in Poole. He had regular stopping places, such as the corner of High Street and Mount Street, and outside Jolliffe House in West Street, so his young customers knew where to find him.

Organ grinder with monkey. This was taken in Green Road, with South Road Girls' School on the left. In winter, he sold hot roast chestnuts outside Beech Hurst in the High Street.

Brownsea, 1960s. The postman seen here emptying a fine Victorian wall post-box on the Island, had to make both collections and deliveries by boat.

Council meeting, *c*. 1900. The Mayor, Sheriff, Town Clerk, Aldermen and Councillors are seated round the Council table at the Guildhall, with the regalia displayed, mace bearers in attendance, and members of the public present.

Mayor's Sunday, 1939. Alderman Joseph Bright was Mayor from 1938 to 1945. The ceremonial route is lined by members of St John's Ambulance Brigade, Poole Fire Brigade and the Poole police force. A contingent of the Dorset Regiment are standing to attention on the right, still wearing puttees as part of their uniform.

Mayor's Sunday, 21 June 1987. On the balcony, left to right: Deputy Mayor (Gerald Bailey, Mayor in 1986), mace bearer (Robin Poulton), Town Clerk (Iain Andrews), Mayor (Randolph Meech), mace bearer (George Wide), Sheriff (Kevin Chaffey, Mayor in 1988), Under-Sheriff (Lewis Parkyn). Councillors are standing on the steps, and officers below.

Mayor with Civic Regalia, *c.* 1880. Born in about 1823, George Curtis was Mayor of Poole in 1879, 1880, 1900 and 1906, as well as serving the town for many years as council member and Alderman. His son Jesse (born in 1846) was Sheriff in 1898. George celebrated his diamond wedding anniversary in 1903 – see p. 43.

Town maces and Mayor, 1951. Miss Margaret Mary Llewellin of Upton House was the first woman to be elected Mayor of Poole, after being its first female Sheriff in 1949. She served as Mayor again in 1953.

Fire engine, 1960s. This old engine was being moved into storage in the New Forest. In February 1993 it was brought to Poole Museum for exhibition.

Opening of Poole's new fire station, 1936. This view of the ceremonial exit of one of the engines and its men was taken from 34 Wimborne Road.

Councillor Reuben White, *c.* 1930. Reuben White had a blacksmith's shop in Mount Street, and for many years drove the horse-drawn fire engine 'Victor' for the brigade.

Fire brigade funeral, 1936. The funeral procession of Reuben White is seen here passing the Wesleyan church in Poole High Street. William Henry Birch is walking behind the hearse in dress uniform, next to the man in a bowler hat.

Towngate Street, 1925. William J. Gould is standing beside his prize-winning Easter window display, which had been dressed by him and his assistant Leslie Poole, who later had his own shop in North Street. *The Stage*, *The Smallholder*, *Boy's Friend*, and *The Scout* are on sale.

Loudspeaker van, 1920s. Radio House supplied loudspeaker equipment for vans, boats, electioneering, sports days, and so on. In 1939 their customers included the armed services, civil defence, and 'Music While You Work' for factories and offices.

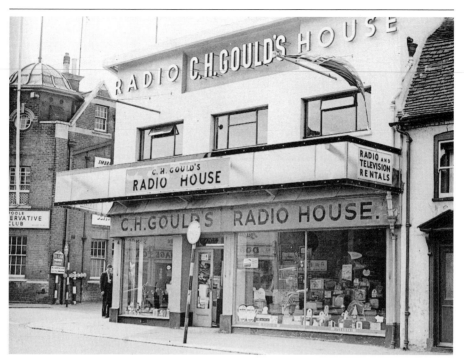

Radio House, 1950s. C.H. Gould founded his radio business in 1922, on the first floor of his father's newspaper shop in Towngate Street. The following year, he took over the shop next door, and in 1928 began a fifty-year association with L.H. Wyatt and John Percy Wills, during which they moved across the road to these premises.

Television demonstration, 1952. This display and demonstration celebrated the opening of Wenvoe 405-line transmitter, and was first held next door – in Tapper's coffin-making room.

Governess cart, *c.* 1905. Charles Cave of Pound Street, a milkman, is about to take his wife and daughter for an afternoon drive.

Ridout's van, *c.* 1900. Several members of the Ridout family were butchers in Poole. Here, Arthur Ridout is delivering orders to customers, as most shops did until about 1960.

Delivery van, *c.* 1900. Messrs W.J. Stickland & Company were wholesale confectioners, trading from Beech House, 18 and 20 Wimborne Road.

Gas vans, *c.* 1910. Bournemouth Gas & Water Company not only advertised the use of coal gas for motor fuel, they practised it – as shown by the large container on the roof of each of these vans.

Mr Bast, May 1903. This wall of work for the billposter includes a sale notice for Chaddesley, Parkstone.

King's Cycle Works, 1903. George Fry persuaded these mechanics to pose for his stereoscopic photograph.

TRANSPORT

Tricycle, c. 1890. This would have been specially
made at a cycle works, such as King's of Poole and
Wimborne. (Family photograph of Mrs Eva Haskins,
née Smith, born 1903, died 3 October 1972.)

Stage coach, *c.* 1905. This coach was hired from the Royal Blue Company for outings and events. Here, it is passing a tram stop, as a tram is about to arrive there. Note the man pulling a bath chair.

Crashed tram, 1 May 1908. From July 1905 Poole Corporation leased its tramway to Bournemouth Corporation, to run a unified service. There were two routes between Poole and Bournemouth, with a connecting service via North Road: the upper along Ashley Road, Parkstone; the lower through Ashley Cross.

Engine number 44826 is seen here in 1955 from the High Street footbridge, heading the London train out of Poole station, which can be seen behind Towngate footbridge, through the smoke.

Horse and cart, *c.* 1910. This outing by Branksome Salvation Army includes Mrs Bale (as a child), and her mother.

Steam wagonette, *c.* 1905. This steam traction engine ran a regular service from the bottom of Evening Hill to Sandbanks, for the Haven Hotel. On the right is James Wilkins, the engineer.

Charabanc, 1930s. The people on this outing are formally dressed, but one small boy in the middle has his bucket and spade.

Motor-cycle, *c*. 1920. In this Methodist tennis group are Reginald George White (of Railway Terrace), back row, third from right, and his future bride Louisa Kelley of Clapper Farm, wearing a striped blazer.

The Land Boundaries Tour. The Society of Poole Men organized a Tour of the Land Boundaries, to complement the seaward excursion.

Submarine, 1919. As part of war reparations, several German submarines were brought to Poole to be scrapped. Crowds flocked to see them: here a party of schoolgirls in uniform is queuing to go below decks.

Schooner yacht, *c.* 1938. *Westward* was a 2,000 ton four-masted yacht owned by H.K. Hales, and moored in Poole Harbour for about three years as a luxury hotel. Here, her flags are flying for Poole Regatta.

Ferry to Hamworthy, 1949–50. Bill Alpens still operated the traditional ferry on demand, or when the lifting bridge was being serviced.

Channel Island ferry, 25 April 1939. Near the High Street junction, people are queuing to board *New Fawn* for the first trip of a new passenger and cargo service between Poole and Guernsey.

Paddle-steamer, *c.* 1912. *Studland Belle* was a 72 ton wooden clinker-built vessel built in 1904. Captain Shippick used her here in 1912 and 1913, until she was destroyed by fire. Her remains were built into the foundations of Poole power station.

Flying boat JW 715 in Poole Harbour, 1940s. BOAC transferred its flying boat operations to Poole Harbour in 1940, remaining here until 1948. During that time, despite wartime difficulties, flights were made to the USA, South Africa, India, Australia and the Far East.

GREATER POOLE

Wimborne Road, 1936. The new central fire station is almost complete. Men are digging

trenches for its connections to main services, without the use of cones or barriers, opposite

the entrance to the stadium.

Seldown allotments, *c.* 1900. These allotments were on what had been mudlands, near the Ladies' Walking Field, and were liable to flooding. The spire of Longfleet Church can be seen on the far right; nearer is a long building belonging to the Pitwines Gas Works. Between that and the gasometer are the chimneys and rooftops of houses and factories near Emerson Road.

Wimborne Road, 1936. Next to the junction with Serpentine Road, no. 39 has become Wessex Tyre Supplies; no. 34 is opposite, on the bend. Most of this area was demolished for a large office building and roundabout.

Longfleet pound, *c.* 1900. Animals found straying in the parish of Longfleet were impounded here, until a fine was paid. Its size indicates that only one or two strays were expected; it was probably much larger in 1850.

Pound sign. This commemorative sign was erected at the Longfleet end of Pound Lane, when the old parish pound was redeveloped.

Clapper Farm, *c.* 1900. Clapper Farm was just below Longfleet Church, as can be seen in this picture, and was worked by the Kelley family; Poole Hospital is now on the site. At one time, its fields stretched from where the stadium now is, to the mudlands which became Poole Park. In this picture are William Kelley, his mother, his wife Alice, brother Fred, and daughter Louisa, with some of their stock.

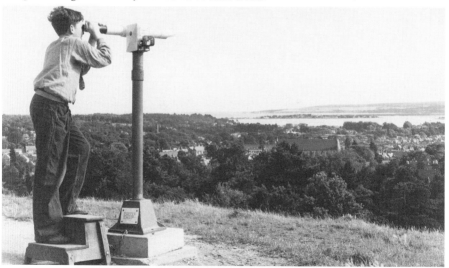

View from Constitution Hill, 1960s. Looking towards the harbour, the roof of St Peter's Church can be seen to the right of centre.

Longfleet in snow, 25 April 1908. This panoramic view from Constitution Hill clearly shows the Purbeck hills beyond the spire of St Mary's Church, Longfleet. The area down to the harbour was known as Brown Bottom.

Parkstone in snow, 25 April 1908. Looking south-east from Constitution Hill, the tram poles in North Road are very noticeable. In 1902, discussing road widening to facilitate the tramway, the Corporation agreed to plant the hill 'to prevent large quantities of sand and earth being washed on to the road'.

Ashley Road, *c*. 1932. This was taken from near 290 Ashley Road, looking west. The tram service ceased in 1935.

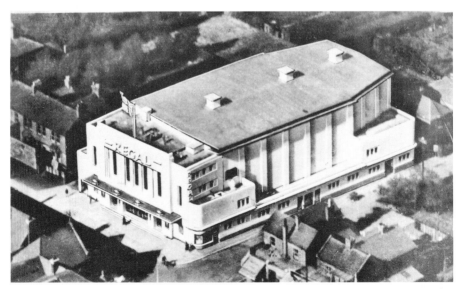

Regal cinema, *c*. 1930. On the corner of Ashley Road and Jubilee Road, Parkstone, this cinema later became a Tesco supermarket, then an Iceland frozen food centre.

Broadstone, *c.* 1910. The golf pavilion and adjacent houses are just north of the old railway junction between the lines of the Somerset & Dorset Joint Railway and the London & South Western Railway, which went to Southampton and Dorchester via Wimborne.

Broadstone, 1950s. Looking towards the railway lines, we can see nos 171–203 The Broadway, with pavement pumps opposite the mature trees. It seems quiet compared with today.

Canford Manor, *c.* 1900. In about 1850 the Guest family settled into their new country seat, after having it altered to their taste. When they bought it, there was little left of the ancient buildings, as its previous owners had rebuilt most of it in Gothic style. One range of buildings remained, known as John O'Gaunt's kitchen, the roof of which can be seen on the right here, behind the cloisters.

John O'Gaunt's kitchen, *c.* 1900. Refitted to accommodate Victorian catering needs, this may have been a medieval great hall.

Canford Mill, *c.* 1900. The mill is situated on the banks of the river Stour, not far from the manor house and church, south of Wimborne.

Canford Magna, *c.* 1900. This was designed as a model village for Lady Wimborne. Nearly two hundred estate cottages were built on similar lines, replacing older homes belonging to the manor, and are locally known as 'Lady Wimborne's cottages'.

Planting a sapling, *c*. 1901. Mr William Llewellin JP watching his younger children John and Margaret help the gardener tread in a sapling at Upton, their new home.

The Llewellin children, *c*. 1902. From the left are William (served with the 4th Dorsets in India during the First World War, MA at Oxford in 1919), John Jestyn (1893–1957, Lord Llewellin), Margaret Mary (first woman to hold civic office in Poole).

Upton House, *c.* 1938. This aerial view shows the house set in its park, with the walled garden to the right of the picture.

Human chess pieces, 1930s. This fête at Upton House was probably talked about for ages afterwards. Chairs have been brought out from the house for the comfort of guests watching this game.

Creekmoor bridge, *c.* 1900. This bridge spanned a tidal inlet of Holes Bay, on what was the main road between Fleetsbridge and Upton before the modern bypass was built.

Creekmoor, 1960s. After this line was made redundant, the stretch from Fleetsbridge to Broadstone became Broadstone Way, part of a new road system linking with Hunger Hill roundabout.

Creekmoor, *c.* 1900. Creekmoor mill and mill house look well tended and prosperous at this time.

Creekmoor mill, 1971. Part of the machinery which drove the mill during its working life lies derelict, and is awaiting removal.

Creekmoor, 1945. During the Second World War, Creekmoor mill and mill house became the headquarters of 15th Platoon of Poole Home Guard, who are seen here before disbandment.

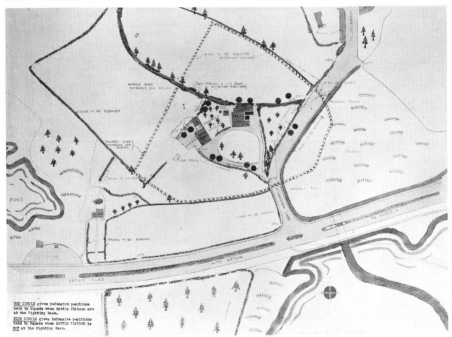

Creekmoor plan, 1939. This plan shows positions to be adopted in the event of invasion. The area is now largely residential.

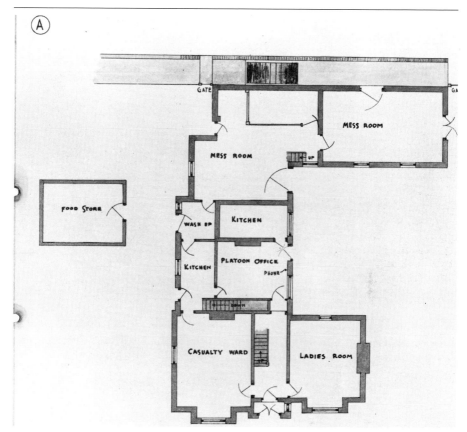

Creekmoor HQ plan, 1939. Drawn by Bill Eason of Poole Pottery, this shows how Poole Home Guard used Creekmoor mill and mill house as headquarters for 15th Platoon.

Hamworthy, c. 1900. On the right is the corner of Lake Road; the shop on the corner became a sub-post office. On the left are St Michael's Church, the Red Lion public house and part of a little corner store.

Lake Farm, Hamworthy, *c*. 1900. This farm was situated in Lake Road, near Lulworth Avenue.

Hamworthy, *c*. 1900. The camera is looking along Carter's Avenue, between Blandford Road and Hamworthy Junction station.

Junction Road, *c.* 1905. These cottages stood near Hamworthy Junction station.

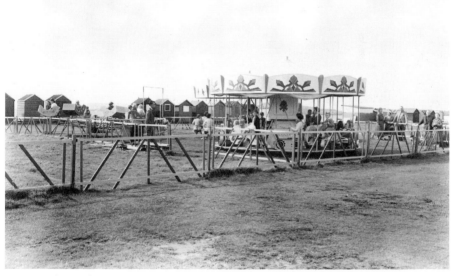

Hamworthy Park, 1960. Between the children's play area and the beach are the only beach huts in the area.

Hamworthy, *c.* 1905. This part of the shore is known as Lake, from the large water-filled clay pit just behind it; it was a popular walking and swimming area.

Rockley Point, *c.* 1960. In the 1950s Rockley Sands Caravan Park was developed near here, and attracted thousands of holidaymakers each year.

Section Ten

A DAY AT THE
SEASIDE

Bathers, c. 1905. The exuberance of the families in this

picture is noticeable; they are too busy enjoying themselves

to pose. But how did the photographer achieve his height?

The water is too shallow for a sizeable boat, and a balloon

or plane would have attracted attention; it must have been

skyhooks.

Hamworthy beach, *c.* 1928. The railway lines between Ballast Quay and the station are just above this little beach, which was the nearest beach to the old town, and very popular with local youngsters and fishermen. It is now part of the Truckline Ferry terminal.

Beach bungalow, 1920s. This beach house at Chaddesley Wood was used extensively by the Hawes family.

Sandbanks, c. 1910. This is the beach below Chaddesley Wood, with steps up to the refreshment kiosk, and early beach huts above the foreshore.

Branksome Chine beach, 1920s. Postmarked 20 July 1924, this photographic card shows the individuality of beach huts at that time. Since then, coastal erosion has been severe along this stretch of sandy cliffs.

Damaged beach huts, 1930s. Winter gales wrecked these popular beach huts near Chaddesley Wood. The Council replaced them, after doing various work to reduce coastal erosion.

Sandbanks beach, *c.* 1939. After terracing the cliff, maisonettes were built in Chaddesley Wood, overlooking the beach.

Chaddesley Glen, 1939. This is a front view of the maisonettes. The scheme was unable to be completed on time, as the builder could not obtain materials once war started.

'The Yam', Shore Road, *c.* 1938. Originally a single-storey building, it was enlarged into a café, as well as a general store and house agency.

BEVERAGES

Tea : Indian or China	per person	4d.
Coffee	-	per cup	3d.
Cocoa	-	,,	3d.
Chocolate	-	,,	4d.
Milk : Cold	-	per glass	2d.
,, Hot	-	,,	3d.
Hot Milk with dash Coffee	,,	4d.
Egg and Milk	-	,,	d.
Horlick's Malted Milk, plain	,,	3d.
,, made with Milk	,,	5d.
Bovril	-	per cup	4d.
,, with Milk	-	,,	6d.
Oxo	-	,,	4d.
Soda Water	-	per glass	3d.
,, and Milk	-	,,	3d.
Lemon or Orange Squash	,,	3d.
,, ,, with Soda	,,	4d.
Mineral Waters	-	,,	4d.

CAKES, TOAST, etc.

Bread and Butter	-	per plate	2d.
Scones (Home-made)	each	1d.
Dry Toast per round		2d.
Hot Buttered ,,		3d.
Cakes	-		2d
Chocolate Biscuits	-		2d.
Biscuits, per portion		2d.
Sandwiches	each	3d.
Jam, Marmalade, Honey, etc.		3d.
Cream	-	-	3d.
Butter	-	-	1d.

TEA TARIFF

Try a

Dorset Tea

consisting of :

TEA
2 SCONES
BUTTER
JAM
CREAM
and
CAKE (Choice)

1/3

LIGHT REFRESHMENTS

EGG DISHES

Boiled Eggs	-	each	d.
Poached Egg on Toast (one)		d.
,, ,, (two)		d.
Egg and Bacon		d.

SAVOURIES

Heinz, Baked Beans on Toast	8d.
,, Spaghetti ,,	8d.
,, ,, and Poached egg	d.
Sardines on Toast (two)	7d.
Soup (various)	6d.
Cheese	-	-	2d.
Pickles	-	-	3d.

FRUITS

Fruit Salad, Apricots, Pears, etc.	6d.
,, ,, with cream	8d.
Fresh Fruit	d.

COLD BUFFET

Ham, Tongue	-	1s.
Salmon, Lobster, Crab	1s.

ICES (April to Sept.)

Vanilla	-	4d., 6d.
Neapolitan	-	6d.
Choc. or Coffee	-	3d.

'The Yam' menu, *c.* 1938. An impressive array of drinks and snacks was available at the cafe.

Postcard, *c.* 1903. It was not until 14 September 1894 that the first picture postcard was posted in Britain; by 1900, two million a day were being posted, and most were delivered the same day.

Crested china, *c.* 1920. Made by Goss, Copeland and other Midland firms, these souvenirs are now collectors' items. The Poole Coat of Arms is on each of these examples.

Acknowledgements

Items included in this book have come into the Photographic Collection of Poole Museum Service from many sources over a long period of time. An important section is the Ernest Bristowe Collection, comprising work by three members of the Bristowe family.

I am pleased to acknowledge permission to publish from Ernest and Barbara Bristowe, Mr R.G. Hawes, Mrs Leeming, Mr and Mrs B. Poole, Mr White, the Trustees of Skinner Street United Reformed Church, Pilkington Tiles Ltd, and the many people who have brought us material in the past with permission to use it when required. Graham M. Smith has kindly given permission for the inclusion of his drawing of Fish Street in Tudor times, one of three he made for the Museum.

My grateful thanks are due to all my colleagues for their help and encouragement, especially to Stephen Courtney for his skill in reviving faded photographs, and his care in copying all our pictures despite difficulties of time and space.

Much of the credit for my interest in and knowledge of Poole's photographic past is due to the infectious enthusiasm, long memories and keen powers of observation shown by Jack and Reg Spinney and the late Les Chisman, who gave their time during the mid-1980s to identifying photographs in the Museum's collection, during my early years as custodian.

I have also had the benefit of past discussions with Iain Andrews, Gordon Clapp, Judy Day, Andrew Hawkes, Dorothy, David and Frank Henson, Pam Mosley, Dorothy Orchard, Ken Standing, Vic Stout, 'Dai' Watkins, Sandy Wills, and many others with knowledge of Poole's history.

Lastly, any errors are my own, and I would be glad to correct them if notified.

BRITAIN IN OLD PHOTOGRAPHS

To order any of these titles please telephone Littlehampton Book Services on 01903 721596

Scunthorpe, *D Taylor*
Skegness, *W Kime*
Around Skegness, *W Kime*

LONDON

Balham and Tooting, *P Loobey*
Crystal Palace, Penge & Anerley, *M Scott*
Greenwich and Woolwich, *K Clark*
Hackney: A Second Selection, *D Mander*
Lewisham and Deptford, *J Coulter*
Lewisham and Deptford: A Second Selection, *J Coulter*
Streatham, *P Loobey*
Around Whetstone and North Finchley, *J Heathfield*
Woolwich, *B Evans*

MONMOUTHSHIRE

Chepstow and the River Wye, *A Rainsbury*
Monmouth and the River Wye, *Monmouth Museum*

NORFOLK

Great Yarmouth, *M Teun*
Norwich, *M Colman*
Wymondham and Attleborough, *P Yaxley*

NORTHAMPTONSHIRE

Around Stony Stratford, *A Lambert*

NOTTINGHAMSHIRE

Arnold and Bestwood, *M Spick*
Arnold and Bestwood: A Second Selection, *M Spick*
Changing Face of Nottingham, *G Oldfield*
Mansfield, *Old Mansfield Society*
Around Newark, *T Warner*
Nottingham: 1944–1974, *D Whitworth*
Sherwood Forest, *D Ottewell*
Victorian Nottingham, *M Payne*

OXFORDSHIRE

Around Abingdon, *P Horn*
Banburyshire, *M Barnett & S Gosling*
Burford, *A Jewell*
Around Didcot and the Hagbournes, *B Lingham*
Garsington, *M Gunther*
Around Henley-on-Thames, *S Ellis*
Oxford: The University, *J Rhodes*
Thame to Watlington, *N Hood*
Around Wallingford, *D Beasley*
Witney, *T Worley*
Around Witney, *C Mitchell*
Witney District, *T Worley*
Around Woodstock, *J Bond*

POWYS

Brecon, *Brecknock Museum*
Welshpool, *E Bredsdorff*

SHROPSHIRE

Shrewsbury, *D Trumper*
Whitchurch to Market Drayton, *M Morris*

SOMERSET

Bath, *J Hudson*
Bridgwater and the River Parrett, *R Fitzhugh*
Bristol, *D Moorcroft & N Campbell-Sharp*
Changing Face of Keynsham,
B Lowe & M Whitehead

Chard and Ilminster, *G Gosling & F Huddy*
Crewkerne and the Ham Stone Villages,
G Gosling & F Huddy
Around Keynsham and Saltford, *B Lowe & T Brown*
Midsomer Norton and Radstock, *C Howell*
Somerton, Ilchester and Langport, *G Gosling & F Huddy*
Taunton, *N Chipchase*
Around Taunton, *N Chipchase*
Wells, *C Howell*
Weston-Super-Mare, *S Poole*
Around Weston-Super-Mare, *S Poole*
West Somerset Villages, *K Houghton & L Thomas*

STAFFORDSHIRE

Aldridge, *J Farrow*
Bilston, *E Rees*
Black Country Transport: Aviation, *A Brew*
Around Burton upon Trent, *G Sowerby & R Farman*
Bushbury, *A Chatwin, M Mills & E Rees*
Around Cannock, *M Mills & S Belcher*
Around Leek, *R Poole*
Lichfield, *H Clayton & K Simmons*
Around Pattingham and Wombourne, *M Griffiths,
P Leigh & M Mills*
Around Rugeley, *T Randall & J Anslow*
Smethwick, *J Maddison*
Stafford, *J Anslow & T Randall*
Around Stafford, *J Anslow & T Randall*
Stoke-on-Trent, *I Lawley*
Around Tamworth, *R Sulima*
Around Tettenhall and Codsall, *M Mills*
Tipton, Wednesbury and Darlaston, *R Pearson*
Walsall, *D Gilbert & M Lewis*
Wednesbury, *I Bott*
West Bromwich, *R Pearson*

SUFFOLK

Ipswich: A Second Selection, *D Kindred*
Around Ipswich, *D Kindred*
Around Mildenhall, *C Dring*
Southwold to Aldeburgh, *H Phelps*
Around Woodbridge, *H Phelps*

SURREY

Cheam and Belmont, *P Berry*
Croydon, *S Bligh*
Dorking and District, *K Harding*
Around Dorking, *A Jackson*
Around Epsom, *P Berry*
Farnham: A Second Selection, *J Parratt*
Around Haslemere and Hindhead, *T Winter & G Collyer*
Richmond, *Richmond Local History Society*
Sutton, *P Berry*

SUSSEX

Arundel and the Arun Valley, *J Godfrey*
Bishopstone and Seaford, *P Pople & P Berry*
Brighton and Hove, *J Middleton*
Brighton and Hove: A Second Selection, *J Middleton*
Around Crawley, *M Goldsmith*
Hastings, *P Haines*
Hastings: A Second Selection, *P Haines*
Around Haywards Heath, *J Middleton*
Around Heathfield, *A Gillet & B Russell*
Around Heathfield: A Second Selection,
A Gillet & B Russell
High Weald, *B Harwood*
High Weald: A Second Selection, *B Harwood*
Horsham and District, *T Wales*

Lewes, *J Middleton*
RAF Tangmere, *A Saunders*
Around Rye, *A Dickinson*
Around Worthing, *S White*

WARWICKSHIRE

Along the Avon from Stratford to Tewkesbury, *J Jeremiah*
Bedworth, *J Burton*
Coventry, *D McGrory*
Around Coventry, *D McGrory*
Nuneaton, *S Clews & S Vaughan*
Around Royal Leamington Spa, *J Cameron*
Around Royal Leamington Spa: A Second Selection,
J Cameron
Around Warwick, *R Booth*

WESTMORLAND

Eden Valley, *J Marsh*
Kendal, *M & P Duff*
South Westmorland Villages, *J Marsh*
Westmorland Lakes, *J Marsh*

WILTSHIRE

Around Amesbury, *P Daniels*
Chippenham and Lacock, *A Wilson & M Wilson*
Around Corsham and Box, *A Wilson & M Wilson*
Around Devizes, *D Buxton*
Around Highworth, *G Tanner*
Around Highworth and Faringdon, *G Tanner*
Around Malmesbury, *A Wilson*
Marlborough: A Second Selection, *P Colman*
Around Melksham,
Melksham and District Historical Association
Nadder Valley, *R. Sawyer*
Salisbury, *P Saunders*
Salisbury: A Second Selection, *P Daniels*
Salisbury: A Third Selection, *P Daniels*
Around Salisbury, *P Daniels*
Swindon: A Third Selection, *The Swindon Society*
Swindon: A Fourth Selection, *The Swindon Society*
Trowbridge, *M Marshman*
Around Wilton, *P Daniels*
Around Wootton Bassett, Cricklade and Purton, *T Sharp*

WORCESTERSHIRE

Evesham to Bredon, *F Archer*
Around Malvern, *K Smith*
Around Pershore, *M Dowty*
Redditch and the Needle District, *R Saunders*
Redditch: A Second Selection, *R Saunders*
Around Tenbury Wells, *D Green*
Worcester, *M Dowty*
Around Worcester, *R Jones*
Worcester in a Day, *M Dowty*
Worcestershire at Work, *R Jones*

YORKSHIRE

Huddersfield: A Second Selection, *H Wheeler*
Huddersfield: A Third Selection, *H Wheeler*
Leeds Road and Rail, *R Vickers*
Pontefract, *R van Riel*
Scarborough, *D Coggins*
Scarborough's War Years, *R Percy*
Skipton and the Dales, *Friends of the Craven Museum*
Around Skipton-in-Craven, *Friends of the Craven Museum*
Yorkshire Wolds, *I & M Sumner*